YOUR KNOWLEDGE HAS VALUE

- We will publish your bachelor's and master's thesis, essays and papers

- Your own eBook and book - sold worldwide in all relevant shops

- Earn money with each sale

Upload your text at www.GRIN.com and publish for free

Zubeda Issa Mohammed

What makes a city "global"?

GRIN Verlag

Bibliografische Information der Deutschen Nationalbibliothek:

Die Deutsche Bibliothek verzeichnet diese Publikation in der Deutschen National-
bibliografie; detaillierte bibliografische Daten sind im Internet über http://dnb.d-
nb.de/ abrufbar.

Imprint:

Copyright © 2012 GRIN Verlag GmbH
Druck und Bindung: Books on Demand GmbH, Norderstedt Germany
ISBN: 978-3-656-74165-7

This book at GRIN:

http://www.grin.com/en/e-book/279988/what-makes-a-city-global

What makes a city "global"?

Nowadays globalization occurs in places where a mass of people work and live in cities. However, for a city to achieve the title of being global, it must have values and ideas that will have an impact of the rest of the world. "Global city is a term that raises an understanding for the cognoscenti" (Low, 2005: p218). Low (2005) further says that a global city is a city that is well thought out to be an important node in the world's economic system. A global city has wealth, power and influence to other countries as well as hosts the largest capital markets. Moreover, a city that has wealthy multinational companies, good infrastructure, better economy, well-educated and diverse populations and powerful organizations as well as a good political structure that are linked to the other parts of the world like nowhere else is considered to be global (Badcock, 2002: p31). A global city, therefore, is the world's most important and influential city that covers the dimensions of the globalization. These dimensions are cultural experience, business activity, human capital as well as political engagement. London, New York, Paris, Rome and Tokyo are one of the most well-known global cities as it provides global competitiveness for its citizens and companies.

There are several ways in which a city can be considered as a global city. Firstly, a city should have a combination of powerful, strong and unique culture, style and history. This is because culture is one of important businesses in a city that provides many tourist attractions. Rome for instance, has been very powerful and influential in the development of world culture. It is one of the richest and dynamic cities in Europe. During the previous years, cultures in Rome have been contained within its borders. However, as the rate of communication increases due to globalization, the culture in Rome is now rapidly mixed on a global scale. A culture may not necessarily mean the traditions and values in that particular city but also the art, food and architecture. Moreover, culture has become an economic machine where by it has a variety of activities through its traditional and modern appeal like the Roman Catholic Church in Rome (Taylor, 2004: p57). In addition, Rome actually influences the world on the subjects of culture, religion and architecture and it is worldwide known as a center of arts. Due to the city's importance and influence in culture and religion, it has been nicknames as the Eternal City of the world (Taylor, 2004: p57). Most importantly fact about Rome is that it is "the main center of pilgrimage in the Christian community" (Taylor, 2004: 56p). Because of the presence of the first Roman Catholic, it has made it to be

1

an influential city since many people especially Christians meet in that area during Easter season to experience and enjoy the traditional procession of the pope. Additionally, for a city to become global, it should have an existence of substantial and vibrant cultural economy with a high level of interconnectedness in the global cultural network. And since the city of Rome and Paris contain world heritage sites, it has a significance being a global city historically and culturally.

Secondly, a global city is a city of demographic and economic change. It contains international organizations, different firms such as law firms, headquarters for the multinational countries as well as stock exchanges that influences the world's economy. Also, in a global city, the cost of living is better than other cities and there are a number of billionaires. For instance New York City, it is the most populous city in the United States of America. It is also the center of international business, a command center in the world's economy and also the main center for business such as legal services, world trade, insurance, banking etc. Due to its increase in the economic growth, New York City has become the largest city in the world in terms of economy (Sassen, 2001: p39). New York City is considered to be a global city because it has powerful organizations that are linked to the other parts and many of the major corporations and multinational companies are headquartered in this city. According to Lipsitz (2010), a global city needs to have a lot of capital, information on trade, business and multinational companies. New York City has all this. Furthermore, New York City made it as a global city because it is considered as a location for one of the major centers of finance and commerce (Lipsitz, 2010). Manhattan, which is one of the districts of New York City, it is the economic heart of the city that contains many headquarters such as the United Nations which has a major influence in the world as well as the stock exchange on the Wall Street. Since the stock market is presence in New York, the city has an advantage of controlling on what goes in and out of the country. Thus, if a problem occurs in New York, it means that it will have an effect on the stock markets globally. For instance during the September attacks, there was an effect on the global economy causing the global stock markets to decrease rapidly and also caused a delay in the opening of the New York's stock exchange when a plane crashed into the World Trade Center building. This shows that a global city has a major influence in other cities as well not just its domain city like when the New York stock exchange delayed, London, which is a global city as well, its stock exchange was evacuated.

Thirdly, the size of a city does not determine a city to be considered as global rather its infrastructure and workforce. Global cities such as Tokyo have good infrastructure and are also advanced in transportation system that has made it to be known as a global city. Tokyo has the advancement of communications infrastructure such as the high-speed communication lines, fiberoptics and fast wifi networks that many multinational corporations around the globe rely on. This has made Tokyo to be known as the world's technology and digital capitals. Besides, Tokyo is also the largest cosmopolitan city in the world (Globalsherpa, 2011). Although the city of Tokyo was almost destroyed during the World War II, the structure remained a unique urban form (Clark, 2003: p235). However, after the war, Tokyo has rebuilt its city with good infrastructure such as motorways, hospitals, railways, schools etc. so as to have a better human capital for its people. According to the 2010 statistics for human capital in the top ten global cities, Tokyo is ranked the seventh. This is because its life expectancy is literally the highest in world and also has abnormally high population with tertiary degrees. Human capital tend to measure how well a city is for its citizens (Clark, 2003: p235). And the higher the human capital of the city, the more likely it is to be considered as a global city.

Lastly, in order for a city to be considered as a global city it should have a good political structure whereby it can influence and participate in world affairs and different international events. For instance in London, it has hosted the SportAccord convention in the year 2011 that raised the capital's economy (Globalsmes, 2011) as well as the international provision against climate change. When a city is engaged politically, it builds a connection in city development.

In addition, in the model of the global cities, there are many competing versions between the cities. Each city wants to be considered as one of the top global cities in the world with high human capital, economic growth, and significance in culture as well as political engagement that will influence other cities in the world as well as to have the capabilities and the power within all cities. All cities may be seen as a city where resources and skills are produced but only one city wants to be known as the main producer. The better well-being of a city in resources, skills as well as economies, the more powerful and successful a city is thus every global city are in competition between another so as to achieve the highest status of being powerful among all other cities. Also, if the city is powerful, it is able to influence globally. According to the Organisation for Economic Co-operation a development (2006), the document states that there is no one size that fits all. Meaning that there no one model of the global city. Cities with higher quality of infrastructure, political engagement and projects that contributes to the economy are highly considered to be a global city thus also creates competitiveness between cities.

In order for a city to obtain the title of being global it must have different values and ideas that will influence and have an impact on the other cities around the world. Although global cities are the ones that can be categorized as best cultural influences with diverse population, fastest growing economy structures as well as good infrastructure, it should also engage in political business. Therefore, as global cities emerge, they become more competitiveness and create network flows of capital and information that link together. Thus they are understood as primarily shaping the flows and interconnectedness and also having a role in defining the world's economy through socio-political, cultural and historical perspectives. These flows and interconnectedness provides global cities the process of global capitalism. Also, for a city to be global, it should have various engines that will influence and have an effect in the world. These engines may be economic growth or change, cultural and political ideas.

Reference

Badcock, B 2002, *Making sense of the cities,* oxford university press, New York.

Clark, D 2003, *Urban world/ Global city*, Routledge, London.

Co-operation a development, 2006, *Competitive cities in the global economy*, viewed on 9 May 20112, (http://www.oecd.org/document/2/0,3746,en_2649_34413_37801602_1_1_1_1,00.html)

Global Sherpa, 2011, *World's Most Global Cities*, viewed on 9 May 2012, (http://www.globalsherpa.org/best-world-city-list)

Lipsitz, A 2010, *New York Ranked Number One Global City*, viewed 9 May 2012, (http://nyulocal.com/national/2010/09/29/new-york-ranked-number-one-global-city/)

Low, SM 2005, *Theorizing the city*, Rutgers university press, London.

Sassen, S 2001, *The global city: New York, London, Tokyo,* Princeton university press, Oxfordshire.

Taylor, P 2004, *World city network: urban analysis*, Routledge, London.

What makes London a global city (2011), viewed on 9 May 2012, (http://www.globalsmes.org/news/index.php?func=detail&detailid=572&catalog=30&lan=en &search_keywords)